THE DADPRENEUR'S GUIDE

Balancing Family Life and Startup Success

Henry Starks

Copyright © 2024 Henry Starks

All rights reserved

The characters and events portrayed in this book are fictitious. Any similarity to real persons, living or dead, is coincidental and not intended by the author.

No part of this book may be reproduced, or stored in a retrieval system, or transmitted in any form or by any means, electronic, mechanical, photocopying, recording, or otherwise, without express written permission of the publisher.

ISBN-13: 9798343096446

Cover design by: Henry Starks
Library of Congress Control Number: 2018675309
Printed in the United States of America

CONTENTS

Title Page
Copyright
Introduction

The Dadpreneur's Guide	1
Chapter 1: The Dadpreneur Mindset	2
Cultivating a Growth-Oriented Perspective	4
Overcoming Challenges with Resilience	6
Chapter 2: Time Management Strategies for Dadpreneurs	8
Creating a Productive Daily Schedule	10
Utilizing Time-Blocking Techniques	12
Chapter 3: Designing Your Home Office	14
Ergonomics and Comfort for Long Hours	16
Tools and Resources for Efficiency	18
Chapter 4: Family-Friendly Business Ideas	20
Exploring Online Business Opportunities	22
Balancing Family Needs with Business Goals	24
Chapter 5: Parenting Tips for Entrepreneurial Dads	26
Integrating Family Time into Your Schedule	28
Teaching Kids About Entrepreneurship	30
Chapter 6: Networking for Busy Fathers	32
Leveraging Online Networking Platforms	34

Attending Events and Meetups	36
Chapter 7: Work-Life Balance Techniques for Dads	38
Practicing Mindfulness and Presence	40
Scheduling Quality Family Activities	42
Chapter 8: Financial Planning for Dad-Led Startups	44
Understanding Business Financing Options	46
Saving for Family and Business Goals	48
Chapter 9: Marketing Strategies for Dadpreneurs	50
Building a Brand That Resonates	52
Utilizing Social Media and Content Marketing	54
Chapter 10: Leveraging Technology to Manage Business and Family	56
Apps for Family Organization	59
Balancing Screen Time with Family Engagement	61
Chapter 11: Personal Development for Entrepreneurial Fathers	63
Continuous Learning and Skill Development	66
Finding Inspiration and Motivation	68
Chapter 12: Celebrating Your Successes and Adjusting Goals	70
Adapting to Life's Changes	72
Planning for the Future with Confidence	74
Entrepreneurship Vibes	77

INTRODUCTION

Being both a father and an entrepreneur often feels like a balancing act. The pressures of running a business while raising a family can leave you feeling stretched thin. *The Dadpreneur's Guide* is here to help you master the art of harmonizing your dual roles. From time management strategies to creating a productive home office, this guide provides practical solutions that empower you to excel in both family life and entrepreneurship.

Through a blend of mindset shifts, time-tested strategies, and real-life stories from fellow dadpreneurs, you'll learn how to stay present for your family while pursuing your entrepreneurial dreams. Whether you're just starting a business or scaling an existing one, this guide will help you strike the perfect balance.

THE DADPRENEUR'S GUIDE

Balancing Family Life and Startup Success

CHAPTER 1: THE DADPRENEUR MINDSET

Embracing the Dual Role of Dad and Entrepreneur

Embracing the dual role of dad and entrepreneur is a journey filled with unique challenges and rewarding moments. As fathers, we often feel the weight of responsibility not just to provide for our families, but also to nurture them. When you add the ambition of building a startup into the mix, it can feel overwhelming. However, by acknowledging the duality of these roles and intentionally weaving them together, we can create a fulfilling life that honors both our entrepreneurial dreams and our commitments as fathers. The key lies in understanding that these roles are not mutually exclusive; instead, they can complement and enhance one another.

Time management becomes a cornerstone of success for dadpreneurs. It's essential to carve out dedicated time for both family and business activities. This means being deliberate about scheduling family dinners, school events, and quality time, alongside your business meetings and work tasks. Using tools like shared calendars and project management apps can help streamline both personal and professional responsibilities. By setting boundaries and prioritizing your time, you can cultivate a routine that fosters productivity while ensuring you remain present in your children's lives. Remember, it's not just about working hard; it's about working smart and making every moment count.

Creating a home office setup that inspires productivity while being family-friendly can significantly impact your ability to balance these roles. Designate a workspace that minimizes distractions and maximizes efficiency, yet is comfortable enough for family interactions. Incorporate elements that remind you of your family's support, like photos or drawings from your children. Additionally, involve your kids in your workspace where appropriate; this can foster an environment of openness and creativity. When your children see you working diligently on your business, it not only sets an example but also allows them to understand the value of entrepreneurship.

Networking is another critical aspect of thriving as a dadpreneur. Engage with other fathers who are navigating similar paths; they can provide insights, share experiences, and offer encouragement. Attend local meetups, online forums, or social media groups dedicated to entrepreneurial dads. Building a support system of like-minded individuals can alleviate feelings of isolation and provide a wealth of resources. These connections can lead to collaborations, mentorship opportunities, and friendships that enhance both your business and personal life.

Lastly, financial planning is the bedrock of any successful startup and a vital concern for fathers. Approach your finances with a family-oriented mindset, ensuring that both your entrepreneurial ventures and family needs are addressed. Seek advice on budgeting, investing, and saving that aligns with your dual responsibilities. This proactive approach not only secures your business's future but also provides peace of mind for your family. By embracing the dual role of dad and entrepreneur, you can create a legacy of resilience, creativity, and love, proving that it's possible to succeed in business while being a devoted father.

CULTIVATING A GROWTH-ORIENTED PERSPECTIVE

Cultivating a growth-oriented perspective is fundamental for dadpreneurs navigating the challenging terrain of balancing family life and entrepreneurial ambitions. This mindset transforms obstacles into opportunities, allowing fathers to embrace the unpredictable nature of startup life while remaining committed to their family's needs. By fostering a growth-oriented perspective, you empower yourself to view setbacks not as failures, but as valuable lessons that can guide you toward future success. This shift in thinking is essential, not only for personal development but also for setting a positive example for your children, teaching them resilience and the importance of perseverance.

To cultivate this mindset, begin by embracing the idea that learning and improvement are continuous processes. As a dadpreneur, you'll face unique challenges that require adaptability and creativity. Instead of being discouraged by setbacks, use them as stepping stones to refine your business approach. This means regularly seeking feedback, being open to change, and investing in your personal growth through courses, workshops, or networking events. Each experience, whether it's a triumph or a struggle, contributes to your overall knowledge and skill set, equipping you to handle the complexities of both family and business life.

Another crucial aspect of a growth-oriented perspective is the importance of setting incremental goals. It's easy to become overwhelmed by the vastness of your aspirations, but breaking them down into manageable milestones allows you to celebrate small victories along the way. This not only boosts your motivation but also illustrates to your children the value of hard work and progress. By integrating family into these goal-setting sessions, you can foster a collaborative spirit where your children feel invested in your entrepreneurial journey, reinforcing the notion that success is a family affair.

Moreover, surrounding yourself with a supportive community can significantly enhance your growth mindset. Engage with fellow dadpreneurs, mentors, or local business groups that understand the unique balance of fatherhood and entrepreneurship. Sharing experiences and learning from others who are on similar paths can provide invaluable insights and encouragement. These connections can also become a source of accountability, ensuring you stay committed to both your business ambitions and your family responsibilities. Remember, collaboration and support are powerful tools in your entrepreneurial toolkit.

Lastly, practice gratitude and reflection as part of your daily routine. Taking time to acknowledge your achievements, no matter how small, reinforces a positive outlook and helps maintain your focus on growth. Encourage your children to join you in this practice, fostering an environment where both you and your family appreciate the journey, not just the destination. This perspective not only enhances your entrepreneurial resilience but also deepens your family bonds, creating a legacy of growth, adaptability, and love that will inspire future generations.

OVERCOMING CHALLENGES WITH RESILIENCE

Overcoming challenges is a fundamental aspect of the dadpreneur journey, where the dual responsibilities of nurturing a family and building a business often collide. Resilience becomes your most valuable ally in this path. Embracing setbacks and viewing them as opportunities for growth can transform obstacles into stepping stones. The road to success is rarely linear; instead, it is filled with unexpected turns that test your commitment to both your family and your entrepreneurial dreams. Each challenge you face provides a chance to model resilience for your children, demonstrating that perseverance is key to achieving one's goals.

As a dadpreneur, you will encounter numerous challenges that can feel overwhelming. Balancing the demands of a startup with the needs of your family requires a strategic approach. Prioritize your tasks and set realistic expectations for yourself. Break down your goals into manageable steps, which allows you to celebrate small victories along the way. This approach not only helps to minimize stress but also reinforces your resolve to succeed. It's essential to communicate with your family about your business aspirations and the inherent challenges, fostering an environment of support and understanding.

In moments of doubt, remember the power of your "why." The driving force behind your entrepreneurial journey often stems from a desire to provide for your family and create a legacy.

Revisit your motivations regularly, reminding yourself of the impact your efforts will have on your loved ones. This clarity can reignite your passion and help you push through the tough times. Surround yourself with a network of fellow dadpreneurs who understand your struggles. Sharing experiences and solutions can provide new perspectives, making it easier to navigate challenges together.

Integrating resilience into your daily routine also means practicing self-care. As busy dads, we often neglect our own well-being in favor of our family and business responsibilities. However, maintaining physical and mental health is essential for sustained resilience. Establish a routine that includes regular exercise, sufficient rest, and quality time with your family. When you take care of yourself, you become better equipped to handle the inevitable stresses of entrepreneurship. This balance creates a solid foundation from which you can approach challenges with a clear mind and renewed energy.

Ultimately, resilience is about embracing the journey, imperfections and all. Each setback provides an opportunity to learn and grow, both as an entrepreneur and as a father. Celebrate your progress, no matter how small, and remember that every dadpreneur faces challenges along the way. By cultivating a resilient mindset, you not only enhance your chances of startup success but also model valuable life lessons for your children. They will learn that perseverance, adaptability, and a positive outlook are essential skills that will serve them well in their own pursuits. With resilience as your guiding principle, you can confidently navigate the delicate balance of family life and entrepreneurship.

CHAPTER 2: TIME MANAGEMENT STRATEGIES FOR DADPRENEURS

Prioritizing Tasks Effectively

Prioritizing tasks effectively is crucial for dadpreneurs who navigate the delicate balance between their burgeoning startups and family responsibilities. The ability to distinguish between what is urgent and what is important can set the foundation for success. Start by creating a clear list of tasks, categorizing them based on deadlines, impact, and resources required. This not only helps in visualizing the workload but also in identifying which tasks can be delegated or postponed. By maintaining an organized approach, you can ensure that your most important responsibilities, both at home and in your business, receive the attention they deserve.

Emphasizing the value of time management, dadpreneurs should adopt strategies that help streamline their daily routines. Techniques such as time blocking can be particularly effective. Designate specific blocks of time for work, family, and personal development. This structured approach not only minimizes distractions but also allows for focused periods of productivity. When you know that you have set time for family activities, you can engage fully, free from the nagging thoughts of unfinished work. This practice fosters a sense of fulfillment, as you honor both your entrepreneurial ambitions and your family commitments.

In the realm of prioritization, learning to say no is a skill that every dadpreneur must master. With numerous demands on your time, it's essential to assess whether each commitment aligns with your goals. This might mean declining invitations to events or outsourcing tasks that do not require your unique expertise. By doing so, you create space for what truly matters: nurturing your startup and spending quality time with your family. Remember, every yes to a task is often a no to something else, so choose wisely to maintain balance in your life.

Leveraging technology can also play a pivotal role in task prioritization. Utilize apps and tools designed for project management, scheduling, and time tracking. These resources can provide insights into how you spend your time and highlight areas for improvement. For instance, setting reminders and deadlines can keep you accountable and help you stay on track with your goals. Moreover, technology can facilitate communication with family, ensuring that everyone is on the same page regarding commitments and expectations. This not only enhances productivity but also strengthens family bonds as you navigate your entrepreneurial journey together.

Ultimately, prioritizing tasks effectively is about aligning your actions with your values. As a dadpreneur, your desire to succeed in business while being present for your family is a noble pursuit. By establishing clear priorities, managing your time wisely, and leveraging resources, you can create a fulfilling life that honors both your entrepreneurial spirit and your role as a dedicated father. Embrace the journey with confidence, knowing that every small step you take towards prioritization contributes to the larger picture of your success, both at home and in your startup.

CREATING A PRODUCTIVE DAILY SCHEDULE

Creating a productive daily schedule is essential for dadpreneurs who juggle the demands of building a startup while nurturing their family life. A well-structured day not only ensures that you allocate time for critical business tasks but also allows you to be present for the moments that matter most with your loved ones. Start by identifying your priorities: set aside time for family, work, and self-care. Consider using a simple grid system to visualize your day, ensuring that each segment reflects your core values and responsibilities. This approach offers clarity and direction, making it easier to stay focused and motivated.

Time blocking can be a powerful technique for dadpreneurs. By dedicating specific blocks of time for different activities, you create a rhythm that enhances productivity. For instance, reserve your most productive hours for high-concentration tasks like strategic planning or coding while scheduling lighter tasks, such as emails or administrative work, for when your energy dips. This not only helps in making the most of your peak performance hours but also minimizes distractions. Remember to carve out time for family dinners or bedtime stories, reinforcing the importance of connectivity and presence in your household.

Incorporating flexibility into your schedule is crucial for managing the unpredictable nature of family life. As a dadpreneur, unexpected events can arise, from a child's sick day to an urgent business matter. Build buffer times between tasks, allowing you to adapt without feeling overwhelmed. This flexibility fosters resilience and enables you to handle challenges with grace. Additionally, involving your family in planning can create a sense of teamwork, where everyone understands the day's flow and feels invested in each other's success.

Leveraging technology can also enhance your scheduling efforts. Utilize apps and tools specifically designed for time management to keep your tasks organized. Digital calendars can help you visualize your day and set reminders for important commitments. Some apps even allow for shared calendars, making it easier for family members to sync their schedules. This not only reduces the friction of communication but also strengthens your family's bond as you collectively navigate through busy days.

Finally, it's essential to regularly reassess your daily schedule to ensure it remains aligned with your evolving goals and family needs. Take time at the end of each week to reflect on what worked and what didn't. Make adjustments as necessary, celebrating your successes and learning from the challenges. By committing to a productive daily schedule, you empower yourself to thrive as both a dad and an entrepreneur, creating a harmonious balance that nurtures your business ambitions while honoring your family life.

UTILIZING TIME-BLOCKING TECHNIQUES

Time-blocking techniques can be a game-changer for dadpreneurs striving to juggle family life and their entrepreneurial ambitions. By intentionally segmenting your day into dedicated blocks of time for specific tasks, you create a structured approach that minimizes distractions and maximizes productivity. This method empowers you to allocate time for your startup activities while ensuring that family commitments are honored and prioritized. Embracing time-blocking allows you to take control of your schedule, transforming chaos into a disciplined routine that fosters both business growth and family connection.

To begin implementing time-blocking, start by assessing your current commitments. Identify the time slots that are consistently available each day. This could be early mornings before the family wakes up, lunch breaks, or evenings after the kids are in bed. Use these times as your dedicated blocks for focused work on your startup. It's essential to recognize that not every block needs to be filled with work; some should be reserved for family activities or personal time. This balance is crucial for maintaining your sanity and ensuring that your relationships thrive alongside your business ambitions.

Once you have identified your available time slots, it's time to prioritize your tasks. Create a list of daily or weekly objectives that are aligned with your startup goals. Each time block should have a clear purpose, whether it's brainstorming new business ideas, networking with potential collaborators, or handling administrative tasks. By clearly defining what you plan to accomplish during each block, you can dive into your work with intention and focus. This clarity helps to reduce overwhelm and enables you to celebrate small wins along the way, reinforcing your motivation to keep pushing forward.

Another key aspect of effective time-blocking is flexibility. Life as a dadpreneur is unpredictable, and it's essential to remain adaptable to changes in your schedule. If a family obligation arises, don't hesitate to shift your blocks around. Perhaps you need to move a work block to the weekend or adjust your evening schedule. Embracing flexibility allows you to remain committed to both your family and your startup without feeling guilty or stressed. Remember, the goal is to create a sustainable routine that honors your responsibilities and dreams, not to enforce a rigid schedule that adds to your stress.

Finally, review and adjust your time-blocking strategy regularly. As your family grows and your business evolves, your time management needs will change. Set aside time each week to reflect on what worked and what didn't. Are there blocks that consistently go unused? Are there time slots that need more attention? By continually refining your approach, you'll create a personalized time management system that not only supports your entrepreneurial ambitions but also enriches your family life. With time-blocking, you can cultivate an environment where your business thrives, and your family flourishes, proving that success is not a zero-sum game—it's a harmonious balance.

CHAPTER 3: DESIGNING YOUR HOME OFFICE

Setting Up a Distraction-Free Workspace

Creating a distraction-free workspace is essential for the modern dadpreneur striving to balance family life and business ambitions. The allure of a home office lies in its flexibility, yet it can quickly turn chaotic without proper organization. Begin by identifying a dedicated space in your home that is exclusively reserved for work. This area should be away from the usual hustle and bustle of family activities, allowing you to immerse yourself fully in your tasks. Whether it's a spare room, a corner in the living room, or even a well-arranged garage, having a designated workspace sets the tone for productivity and focus.

Next, equip your workspace with essential tools that enhance your efficiency. Invest in a comfortable chair and desk that suit your body and working style. Ergonomics play a vital role in how you feel throughout the day, and comfort can significantly boost your productivity. Additionally, ensure you have all necessary technology at hand, from a reliable computer to high-speed internet, as these are crucial for managing your startup effectively. With the right tools in place, you can minimize interruptions and maximize your output, creating a more effective work environment.

To further reduce distractions, establish clear boundaries with family members regarding your work hours. Communicate your schedule to your partner and children, so they understand when you are available and when you need uninterrupted time. This not only respects your work commitments but also teaches children the importance of boundaries and focus. Involving your family in this process can foster a supportive environment where everyone understands the significance of your entrepreneurial journey while ensuring they feel valued and included.

Incorporating elements that inspire creativity and motivation can also enhance your workspace. Surround yourself with items that remind you of your goals—motivational quotes, pictures of your family, or even artwork that resonates with your entrepreneurial spirit. These visual cues can serve as reminders of why you are working hard and help to maintain your drive. Moreover, consider adding plants or natural elements to your workspace; studies have shown that greenery can boost mood and productivity, making your space feel more inviting and less sterile.

Finally, prioritize maintaining organization within your workspace. Clutter can lead to mental chaos, making it difficult to concentrate. Implement a filing system for important documents, keep your desk tidy, and regularly assess what items are necessary for your work. Use tools like digital calendars or task management apps to keep track of your daily responsibilities, ensuring that you can transition smoothly between family time and work tasks. By fostering an organized and distraction-free workspace, you empower yourself to achieve your business goals while being present for your family, creating a harmonious balance that every dadpreneur aspires to attain.

ERGONOMICS AND COMFORT FOR LONG HOURS

Creating a workspace that prioritizes ergonomics and comfort is essential for dadpreneurs who often find themselves working long hours. As you juggle the demands of building a startup and being present for your family, the importance of a well-designed home office cannot be overstated. An ergonomic setup not only enhances productivity but also protects your health by minimizing strain and discomfort. When you invest in your workspace, you're not just investing in your business but also in your well-being and ability to be there for your loved ones.

Start by evaluating your desk and chair. An adjustable chair that supports your lower back can make a significant difference in how you feel after a long day of work. Pair it with a desk that allows you to alternate between sitting and standing, which can help alleviate fatigue. Consider adding a footrest if your feet don't comfortably reach the ground. By ensuring that your workstation is tailored to your body's needs, you're setting yourself up for success, both in your entrepreneurial endeavors and your role as a father.

Lighting plays a crucial role in creating a comfortable work environment. Natural light is ideal, so position your desk near a window if possible. If that's not an option, invest in adjustable LED lights that mimic daylight and reduce eye strain. A well-lit space not only boosts your mood but also enhances your focus, allowing you to tackle tasks more efficiently. As you embrace these changes, remember that a comfortable workspace fosters creativity and innovation, vital components for any dadpreneur looking to make their mark.

Don't forget about the technology you use daily. Ergonomic keyboards and mice can significantly reduce wrist strain, while monitor stands can help position your screens at eye level, preventing neck and back pain. Incorporating these tools into your setup not only improves comfort but also encourages longer, more productive work sessions. The less you struggle with physical discomfort, the more mental energy you can dedicate to building your business and connecting with your family.

Lastly, take regular breaks to stretch, move around, and recharge. Integrating short breaks into your work routine can combat fatigue and boost your overall productivity. Use this time to engage with your family, even if it's just for a few moments. This balance will keep you connected with your loved ones while reinforcing the importance of self-care. By prioritizing ergonomics and comfort in your workspace, you're not only enhancing your performance as a dadpreneur but also modeling healthy habits for your children, showing them that success is about more than just hard work.

TOOLS AND RESOURCES FOR EFFICIENCY

In the journey of a dadpreneur, having the right tools and resources can make all the difference. The modern entrepreneur is blessed with a plethora of options that can help streamline processes and enhance productivity without sacrificing precious family time. From project management software to communication apps, the right toolkit can empower dads to stay organized and focused, ensuring that both work and family life thrive. By leveraging these tools, you can create a seamless integration between your business aspirations and your family obligations, ultimately leading to a more fulfilling life.

Time management is a critical skill for any dadpreneur, and various resources can aid in this area. Tools like digital calendars, task management apps, and time-tracking software are invaluable for planning your day effectively. These resources not only help you allocate time for work tasks but also ensure you carve out moments for family engagement. By prioritizing your tasks and setting specific goals, you can enhance your efficiency, allowing more time for your loved ones. Embracing these technologies can help you maintain accountability and achieve a balanced approach to your dual roles.

Creating an effective home office setup is another essential aspect of being a successful dadpreneur. A designated workspace can boost productivity and help you maintain a clear division between work and family time. Invest in ergonomic furniture, reliable technology, and adequate lighting to create an environment conducive to focus and creativity. Additionally, consider incorporating elements that remind you of your family, such as photos or drawings from your children. This personal touch can serve as a daily inspiration, reinforcing your motivation to succeed in both your business and family life.

Networking is a powerful tool that can open doors and create opportunities for growth. For busy fathers, finding time to connect with other professionals and potential mentors can be challenging, but it is essential. Online communities, social media groups, and virtual networking events can provide a platform to exchange ideas, seek advice, and collaborate with like-minded individuals. Engaging with fellow dadpreneurs not only expands your professional circle but also provides a support system where you can share your unique challenges and triumphs. Through these connections, you can gain insights that could propel your business forward while fostering a sense of camaraderie.

Lastly, investing in personal development is crucial for entrepreneurial fathers. Books, podcasts, and online courses can equip you with the latest strategies in marketing, financial planning, and work-life balance techniques. Continuous learning enables you to adapt and thrive in the ever-evolving business landscape while also modeling the importance of growth to your children. By prioritizing your own development, you not only enhance your skill set but also set an inspiring example for your family, demonstrating that with commitment and the right resources, it is possible to achieve success in both your personal and professional life.

CHAPTER 4: FAMILY-FRIENDLY BUSINESS IDEAS

Identifying Your Skills and Passion

Identifying your skills and passions is the first critical step for any dadpreneur looking to build a successful startup while maintaining a fulfilling family life. As fathers, we often wear multiple hats, juggling responsibilities at home and ambitions in business. The key to thriving in both realms lies in understanding what you are truly passionate about and recognizing the unique skills you bring to the table. Take some time to reflect on your past experiences, both personal and professional. Consider the activities that energize you and the tasks that make you lose track of time. These reflections can serve as a compass guiding you toward a business idea that resonates with your core values and interests.

Once you've pinpointed your passions, it's vital to assess your skills honestly. This involves a thorough inventory of your abilities—both soft skills, like communication and leadership, and hard skills, such as technical expertise or marketing knowledge. Think about the roles you have held in your career and the moments when you've felt most competent and fulfilled. Don't hesitate to seek feedback from family and friends, as they can offer valuable insights into the strengths they see in you. This self-assessment will not only boost your confidence but also help you align your business concept with your capabilities, increasing the likelihood of success.

It's important to remember that your passions and skills can intersect in unique ways, creating opportunities for innovative business ideas. For instance, if you love cooking and have a knack for social media, consider starting a blog or video channel that showcases family-friendly recipes. This not only allows you to engage in something you love but also makes room for building a community around your interests. Similarly, if you have experience in project management and a passion for parenting, you might develop a coaching service aimed at helping other dads manage their time and priorities more effectively. The possibilities are endless when you allow your skills and passions to inform one another.

In the process of identifying your skills and passions, it's crucial to embrace a growth mindset. Understand that your journey as a dadpreneur will involve learning and adapting. As you delve deeper into your interests, you may discover new skills that you want to develop or refine. Engaging in courses, workshops, or even online communities can provide you with the knowledge and support needed to evolve your capabilities. This commitment to personal development not only enhances your business prospects but also sets a powerful example for your children about the importance of lifelong learning and resilience.

Ultimately, identifying your skills and passions is about creating a roadmap that aligns your entrepreneurial aspirations with your family values. By focusing on what you truly enjoy and what you excel at, you can craft a business that not only generates income but also enriches your time with your family. As you embark on this journey, remember that the most successful dadpreneurs are those who remain authentic to themselves and their families. With clarity about your skills and passions, you can build a startup that reflects your identity as both a father and an entrepreneur, leading to a more balanced and fulfilling life.

EXPLORING ONLINE BUSINESS OPPORTUNITIES

Exploring online business opportunities can be a transformative journey for dads looking to balance the demands of family life with entrepreneurial aspirations. In this digital age, the possibilities are virtually limitless, allowing fathers to create income streams that align with their values and family commitments. The beauty of the online business landscape is its flexibility, enabling you to carve out a niche that resonates with your interests while being present for those precious family moments. With the right mindset and approach, you can build a successful venture that complements your role as a father.

Starting an online business requires a strategic approach, particularly for busy dads who juggle multiple responsibilities. Time management becomes a crucial skill, and utilizing tools like project management software can help you prioritize tasks effectively. Setting aside dedicated time for business activities, even if it's just a few hours a week, can create momentum and foster growth. By clearly defining your goals and breaking them down into manageable steps, you can navigate the transition from corporate life to entrepreneurship without feeling overwhelmed, ensuring that you remain engaged with your family throughout the process.

Choosing the right business model is essential for a dadpreneur. Consider the family-friendly business ideas that align with your passions and expertise. Whether it's launching an e-commerce store, providing digital marketing services, or creating educational content, the options are abundant. Focus on ventures that allow for scalability and can be managed from home. This not only helps you maintain a work-life balance but also provides an opportunity to involve your children in the process, instilling entrepreneurial values and skills in the next generation.

Networking is another vital aspect of exploring online business opportunities. Building connections with other dadpreneurs can provide support, inspiration, and collaboration opportunities. Utilize social media platforms, online forums, and local meetups to connect with like-minded fathers who understand the unique challenges and rewards of balancing family and business. Engaging with a community of entrepreneurial dads can lead to valuable insights, partnerships, and mentorship, all while reinforcing the importance of family in your journey.

Finally, leveraging technology to manage both your business and family life can significantly enhance your productivity. From scheduling tools that help you allocate time for work and family activities to apps that streamline business operations, technology can be your ally. Embrace the resources available to create a harmonious balance between your entrepreneurial ambitions and your role as a father. As you explore online business opportunities, remember that your journey is not just about financial success but also about creating a legacy that empowers your family and inspires your children to pursue their dreams.

BALANCING FAMILY NEEDS WITH BUSINESS GOALS

Balancing family needs with business goals is a challenge that many dadpreneurs face, yet it is a challenge filled with potential for growth and fulfillment. As fathers embark on their entrepreneurial journeys, they often find themselves navigating a landscape where family responsibilities and business ambitions intersect. The key to thriving in this dual role lies in creating a harmonious blend of both worlds. It starts with establishing clear priorities that reflect both personal values and professional aspirations. When dadpreneurs align their business goals with family needs, they not only foster a supportive home environment but also cultivate a thriving business that resonates with their core beliefs.

Time management emerges as a crucial skill for dadpreneurs striving to balance their roles. Utilizing effective time management strategies enables fathers to carve out dedicated hours for their startup while ensuring they are present for family moments that matter. By adopting techniques such as time blocking and prioritizing tasks, dadpreneurs can create a structured schedule that accommodates business meetings, project work, and quality family time. This intentional approach not only enhances productivity but also reinforces the message to family members that their time is valued, ultimately fostering a sense of teamwork and shared purpose.

Creating a family-friendly business model can significantly enhance the ability to balance these two vital aspects of life. Dadpreneurs should consider business ideas that promote flexibility and allow for parental involvement, such as online services or products that can be managed remotely. This not only provides the opportunity to generate income but also facilitates deeper engagement with family life. By designing a business that aligns with family values, dadpreneurs can ensure that their entrepreneurial pursuits do not come at the expense of family connections, but rather enhance them.

Networking plays an essential role in the success of a dadpreneur, and cultivating connections with like-minded individuals can provide both support and inspiration. Engaging with other father entrepreneurs can lead to valuable insights, mentorship opportunities, and collaborative ventures that strengthen both business and personal life. By participating in parenting groups, attending local networking events, or leveraging online platforms, dadpreneurs can expand their networks while sharing experiences and strategies for balancing their dual commitments. This sense of community not only alleviates feelings of isolation but also reinforces the idea that it is possible to pursue ambitious goals while being a present father.

Ultimately, the journey of a dadpreneur is one of personal growth and transformation. Embracing the mindset that both family and business can flourish together empowers fathers to redefine success. By prioritizing family needs alongside business goals, implementing effective time management, creating a family-friendly business, and building supportive networks, dadpreneurs can navigate the complexities of their roles with confidence and passion. This balance not only allows for entrepreneurial success but also enriches family life, fostering deep connections and cherished memories that will last a lifetime.

CHAPTER 5: PARENTING TIPS FOR ENTREPRENEURIAL DADS

Building Strong Family Bonds

Building strong family bonds is essential for every dadpreneur striving to achieve success in both family life and business. As you embark on your entrepreneurial journey, remember that your family is your foundation. By nurturing these relationships, you not only create a supportive environment but also instill values and life lessons that will benefit your children for years to come. Prioritizing family time amidst the hustle of building a startup can be challenging, but with intentional effort, you can foster connections that will strengthen your family unit and provide motivation to excel in your business endeavors.

Creating dedicated family time is a crucial step in building strong bonds. Schedule regular family activities that everyone can look forward to, whether it's a weekly game night, outdoor adventures, or simple dinners together. These moments become cherished memories and offer a break from the pressures of work. As a busy dad, you can incorporate your children into your entrepreneurial journey, inviting them to participate in age-appropriate tasks that help them understand your work. This not only teaches them valuable skills but also allows them to feel included in your life, reinforcing the idea that family comes first.

Open communication is another vital component in strengthening family ties. As you navigate the demands of your startup, ensure that you set aside time to discuss your day, share challenges, and celebrate successes with your family. This transparency fosters trust and understanding, allowing your children and partner to feel they are part of your journey. Encourage your family members to express their thoughts and feelings, creating a safe space where everyone feels heard. This two-way dialogue not only enhances your relationships but also provides you with insights that can help you in your entrepreneurial pursuits.

Balancing work and family life requires you to be present in both realms. Embrace technology as a tool to enhance your efficiency, but be mindful of its potential to distract you from your family. Set boundaries for work hours, and when it's family time, be fully engaged. Put away your devices and focus on building quality interactions. This commitment demonstrates to your children that they are your priority, reinforcing the importance of relationships over work. Remember, your actions speak louder than words; showing up for your family is just as crucial as meeting deadlines for your business.

Finally, don't hesitate to seek support from your partner and other dads in your network. Share your experiences and learn from one another, as collaboration can provide fresh perspectives and encouragement. Whether it's exchanging parenting tips or discussing business strategies, these connections can help you grow both personally and professionally. Building strong family bonds not only enriches your life but also creates a robust support system that empowers you to thrive as a dadpreneur, showing your children the importance of hard work, resilience, and the beauty of balancing business with family.

INTEGRATING FAMILY TIME INTO YOUR SCHEDULE

Integrating family time into your schedule is not just a luxury but a necessity for dadpreneurs striving to find harmony between their business aspirations and family obligations. As a father and entrepreneur, it's essential to recognize that the time spent with your loved ones can fuel your creative energy and provide the emotional support needed to navigate the ups and downs of startup life. By intentionally carving out moments for family, you can create a nurturing environment that encourages both personal and professional growth.

To begin, consider utilizing simple yet effective time management strategies that prioritize family interactions. Start by assessing your weekly schedule and identifying blocks of time that can be dedicated to family activities. Whether it's a Sunday afternoon picnic or a weekday dinner, these scheduled moments serve as anchors in your week, ensuring that family time remains a non-negotiable aspect of your life. The act of planning these moments not only reflects your commitment to family but also sets a positive example for your children about the importance of balancing responsibilities.

In addition to scheduled family activities, leverage technology to enhance your availability. Many dadpreneurs find that tools like shared calendars and communication apps can keep everyone in the loop regarding family events and schedules. By integrating these tools into your daily routine, you can synchronize work commitments with family priorities, making it easier to adjust your plans as needed. This proactive approach not only minimizes conflict but also demonstrates to your children that family is a priority, even amidst the hustle of entrepreneurship.

Moreover, it's crucial to establish boundaries that protect family time from work intrusions. This might involve designating specific hours when work is off-limits, allowing you to engage fully with your family without distractions. Communicate these boundaries to your team and clients, reinforcing that while you are dedicated to your business, your family is equally important. This commitment not only fosters a healthier work-life balance but also cultivates a supportive atmosphere at home, where your family feels valued and appreciated.

Finally, remember that integrating family time into your schedule is an evolving process. It requires reflection and flexibility to adapt as your business grows and your family dynamics change. Embrace the journey, remain open to adjustments, and continuously seek opportunities to deepen your connections with your loved ones. By prioritizing family time alongside your entrepreneurial ambitions, you not only enrich your own life but also lay the foundation for a legacy of balanced success that your children can admire and aspire to emulate.

TEACHING KIDS ABOUT ENTREPRENEURSHIP

Teaching kids about entrepreneurship is not just about instilling business acumen; it's about nurturing a mindset that encourages creativity, resilience, and problem-solving. As Dadpreneurs, we have a unique opportunity to share our journeys with our children, turning everyday experiences into valuable lessons. Whether you're brainstorming a new product or managing your time between family and business, involving your kids can spark their curiosity and inspire them to think like entrepreneurs. This engagement is not just educational; it's a bonding experience that strengthens family ties while planting the seeds of entrepreneurial spirit.

Start by integrating entrepreneurial concepts into fun, everyday activities. Simple games like setting up a lemonade stand can teach kids about sales, customer service, and the importance of understanding their audience. Encourage them to come up with their own product ideas, fostering creativity and critical thinking. Discuss the components of a business plan in a way that's relatable, perhaps by comparing it to planning a family vacation. This way, they learn about budgeting, resource allocation, and goal setting in a context they understand. By making these lessons enjoyable, you're cultivating a passion for entrepreneurship that can last a lifetime.

As you balance your startup journey with family obligations, let your children see the challenges and triumphs you face. Share stories about failures and how you turned them into learning opportunities. This transparency teaches resilience and the value of perseverance. It's essential for kids to understand that setbacks are a natural part of any business endeavor. When they see you adapting to challenges, they learn that determination and flexibility are key traits of successful entrepreneurs. This real-world insight is far more impactful than any textbook lesson.

Encourage your children to set their own goals, whether it's saving for a special toy or starting their small venture. Help them track their progress and celebrate their achievements, no matter how small. This process instills a sense of ownership and accountability while teaching them how to plan and execute ideas. You can also introduce them to the concept of networking by involving them in family or community events where they can meet new people. These interactions will help them understand the importance of building relationships, a crucial skill for any entrepreneur.

Ultimately, teaching kids about entrepreneurship is about more than just business skills; it's about fostering an entrepreneurial mindset that will serve them throughout their lives. By integrating these lessons into your daily routine, you create an environment where innovation and creativity thrive. As Dadpreneurs, we have the privilege of shaping the next generation of thinkers and doers. By balancing our responsibilities and sharing our entrepreneurial journeys, we not only enrich our children's lives but also build a legacy of resilience and creativity that will empower them in their future endeavors.

CHAPTER 6: NETWORKING FOR BUSY FATHERS

Building a Supportive Community

Building a supportive community is essential for any dadpreneur striving to balance the demands of family life and the challenges of starting a business. As fathers, we often find ourselves caught in the tension between nurturing our families and pursuing our entrepreneurial dreams. Creating a network of like-minded individuals can provide the encouragement and resources necessary to navigate this intricate journey. By surrounding ourselves with supportive peers, we cultivate an environment where collaboration flourishes, and shared experiences become a source of inspiration.

One of the most powerful aspects of building a supportive community is the opportunity for mentorship. Connecting with other dads who have successfully balanced family and business responsibilities can offer invaluable insights. These mentors can share practical advice on managing time effectively, setting up an efficient home office, and finding family-friendly business ideas that resonate with both personal values and market needs. Their experiences can illuminate the path forward, helping you sidestep potential pitfalls while gaining confidence in your entrepreneurial endeavors.

Networking with fellow dads also fosters a sense of accountability. When you surround yourself with individuals who understand your unique struggles, you create an environment that motivates you to stay on track. Regular meet-ups, whether virtual or in-person, can serve as checkpoints for your goals. Sharing your progress and challenges with others not only strengthens your resolve but also opens the door to collaborative opportunities. As you share ideas and resources, you may find partners for projects or even new avenues for income generation that align with your family priorities.

In addition to mentorship and accountability, a supportive community can enhance your personal development. Engaging with diverse perspectives helps expand your understanding of various aspects of entrepreneurship, from marketing strategies tailored for dadpreneurs to leveraging technology for seamless family-business integration. Workshops, seminars, or informal gatherings can be excellent platforms for learning and growth, allowing you to hone skills that will benefit both your startup and your role as a father.

Ultimately, building a supportive community is about creating connections that enrich both your personal and professional life. It is a reminder that you do not have to walk this path alone. By actively participating in a network of fellow dadpreneurs, you cultivate a rich tapestry of relationships that empower you to thrive. As you nurture these connections, you not only enhance your chances of startup success but also model the importance of community and collaboration for your children, teaching them that together, we can achieve so much more.

LEVERAGING ONLINE NETWORKING PLATFORMS

In today's digital age, online networking platforms have become invaluable resources for dads embarking on their entrepreneurial journeys. These platforms not only provide a space to connect with like-minded individuals but also serve as fertile grounds for collaboration, idea sharing, and support. For dads who are balancing family responsibilities with the demands of starting a business, utilizing these networks can play a crucial role in building a successful venture while ensuring family time remains a priority.

One of the most significant advantages of online networking is the ability to connect with fellow dadpreneurs who understand the unique challenges of juggling a startup and family life. Platforms such as LinkedIn, Facebook Groups, and specialized forums offer spaces for fathers to share experiences, seek advice, and find mentorship. Engaging with other dads who are navigating similar paths can provide not only motivation but also practical insights that can help streamline your journey, from time management tips to marketing strategies that resonate with a family-oriented audience.

As you build your network, consider actively participating in discussions, sharing your expertise, and showcasing your entrepreneurial journey. This not only establishes you as a valuable member of the community but also opens doors for potential partnerships and collaborations. By providing support and value to others, you cultivate relationships that can lead to business opportunities, referrals, and even friendships. Remember, the strength of your network lies in the quality of connections you make, so invest time in nurturing these relationships.

Moreover, online networking platforms often host events, webinars, and workshops that cater specifically to entrepreneurial fathers. These events can be an excellent way to gain knowledge, refine your skills, and stay updated on industry trends while meeting others who share your aspirations. Even if your schedule is tight due to family commitments, many of these events are recorded or held during off-hours, allowing you to participate without compromising your family time. This flexibility is key for busy dads looking to enhance their professional capabilities without sacrificing their responsibilities at home.

Ultimately, leveraging online networking platforms can significantly enhance your journey as a dadpreneur. By connecting with a supportive community, sharing your experiences, and accessing valuable resources, you can navigate the complexities of building a business while remaining present for your family. Embrace these digital connections, and remember that the journey of entrepreneurship is not one you have to face alone; together, we can create a thriving ecosystem that supports the aspirations of fathers everywhere.

ATTENDING EVENTS AND MEETUPS

Attending events and meetups can be a transformative experience for dadpreneurs seeking to strike a balance between family life and startup ambitions. Engaging with like-minded individuals allows you to share experiences, gather insights, and build a supportive network that understands the unique challenges of juggling responsibilities as a father and entrepreneur. These gatherings provide not only inspiration but also practical strategies that can help you navigate your dual roles more effectively. Embracing the opportunity to connect with fellow fathers who are on similar journeys can ignite your passion and reinforce your commitment to both your family and your business.

Networking at events is more than just exchanging business cards; it's about cultivating relationships that can lead to collaboration and mentorship. As a busy professional transitioning from a corporate job to a business, you may feel overwhelmed by the thought of building connections. However, these meetups are designed for individuals just like you, eager to share their stories and learn from one another. By participating in discussions, workshops, and informal conversations, you can gain valuable insights into time management techniques, financial planning, and marketing strategies tailored for dadpreneurs. The relationships you build can provide support as you navigate the challenges of entrepreneurship while remaining present for your family.

Moreover, events and meetups often feature speakers who are

experienced entrepreneurs and fathers themselves. Their stories of triumphs and setbacks can serve as powerful motivators, reminding you that you are not alone in your journey. Hearing firsthand accounts of how other dads have successfully launched their businesses while maintaining strong family connections can provide you with the encouragement to take bold steps in your own venture. These inspirational narratives can help you visualize the possibilities, encouraging you to embrace the challenges with confidence and determination.

In addition to personal growth, attending these gatherings can enhance your business acumen. Workshops and panel discussions often cover topics such as leveraging technology to manage your business and family life, essential for dadpreneurs striving for efficiency. You will learn about tools and resources that can streamline operations, allowing you to maximize your productivity while still having quality time with your loved ones. By integrating these strategies into your daily routine, you can create a harmonious balance that respects both your entrepreneurial ambitions and your family commitments.

Finally, remember that the journey of a dadpreneur is not a solo endeavor; it thrives on community and shared experiences. By actively participating in events and meetups, you contribute to a larger narrative of fathers who are redefining success on their own terms. Embrace the connections you make, the lessons you learn, and the camaraderie you foster. Your commitment to your family and business can inspire others, creating a ripple effect that encourages more dads to pursue their entrepreneurial dreams without sacrificing what truly matters. Let these gatherings be a source of inspiration, knowledge, and lasting relationships that empower you to thrive as a dadpreneur.

CHAPTER 7: WORK-LIFE BALANCE TECHNIQUES FOR DADS

Establishing Boundaries Between Work and Family

Establishing boundaries between work and family is essential for dadpreneurs striving for success in both realms. As you embark on the journey of building a startup, it's crucial to recognize that your time and energy are finite resources. Setting clear boundaries helps you protect family time while also ensuring that your business objectives are met. By defining specific work hours and creating a dedicated workspace at home, you can foster a productive environment that minimizes distractions and maximizes focus. This conscious separation allows you to engage fully with your family when you're off the clock, nurturing relationships that are foundational to your overall happiness and success.

One of the most effective strategies for maintaining these boundaries is to communicate openly with your family about your work commitments. Let your loved ones know your schedule, including when you'll be working and when you'll be available for family activities. This transparency not only sets expectations but also fosters a sense of teamwork within the household. When your family understands your ambitions and the dedication required to achieve them, they are more likely to respect your working hours and support your entrepreneurial journey. By engaging in regular family discussions, you can also create a shared vision that aligns your entrepreneurial goals with family aspirations.

Integrating technology can further enhance your ability to establish boundaries. Utilize tools that help you manage your time effectively, such as calendar apps that block out work periods and family time. Setting reminders for breaks can help you step away from work and reconnect with your family. Additionally, consider implementing productivity techniques like the Pomodoro Technique, which encourages focused work intervals followed by short breaks. This not only boosts your efficiency during work hours but also ensures that you carve out moments to engage with your family throughout the day.

Flexibility is another vital component of boundary-setting. As a dadpreneur, you may need to adapt to the unpredictable nature of both family life and business. Embrace the idea that boundaries can be fluid, allowing for adjustments when necessary. For instance, if a family event overlaps with a business obligation, consider rescheduling your work commitments or delegating tasks to ensure you remain present for your loved ones. This adaptability not only strengthens your role as a father but also teaches your children valuable lessons about balancing responsibilities and valuing relationships.

Ultimately, setting boundaries is not about creating rigid partitions between work and family; it's about cultivating harmony between your roles as an entrepreneur and a father. By prioritizing both your business ambitions and familial connections, you can create a life that is fulfilling on multiple levels. Remember that success as a dadpreneur is not solely measured by financial gain but also by the quality of the relationships you nurture along the way. Building a thriving business while being a present and engaged father is not only possible but profoundly rewarding when approached with intention and care.

PRACTICING MINDFULNESS AND PRESENCE

Practicing mindfulness and presence is essential for dadpreneurs navigating the intricate dance between family life and startup aspirations. In the hustle of building a business, it is easy to become consumed by tasks, deadlines, and the constant pressure to succeed. Mindfulness serves as a powerful antidote, allowing fathers to cultivate a deeper awareness of their thoughts and feelings, enhancing their ability to engage fully with both their family and their entrepreneurial journey. By incorporating mindfulness practices into daily routines, dadpreneurs can create a foundation of mental clarity and emotional resilience that strengthens their roles as both parents and business leaders.

One effective way to practice mindfulness is through short, intentional moments of reflection throughout the day. This could mean taking five minutes to breathe deeply before diving into work or enjoying a quiet moment with your child, fully present and engaged. These small pauses can help to reset your mind, bringing you back to the moment and allowing you to appreciate the joy of fatherhood amidst the busyness of entrepreneurship. By dedicating time to be present, you not only enhance your ability to make sound decisions in your business but also deepen your connection with your family.

In addition to these brief moments of reflection, creating a dedicated mindfulness practice can significantly benefit dadpreneurs. Whether it's through meditation, yoga, or simply a daily walk in nature, establishing a routine that prioritizes mindfulness can help to reduce stress and improve focus. Engaging in these practices regularly can create a mental space where creativity flourishes, allowing you to approach problems with a fresh perspective. As you become more attuned to your thoughts and emotions, you'll find it easier to navigate the challenges of startup life while remaining available for your family.

Incorporating mindfulness into family activities can also enhance the quality of your time together. Engaging in mindful play with your children—such as being fully present during a game or focusing on the sights and sounds during a nature walk—can strengthen your bond and create lasting memories. This intentional presence not only enriches family life but also sets a positive example for your children, teaching them the value of mindfulness and emotional awareness. As you foster an environment of presence, you cultivate a family culture that values connection, understanding, and support.

Ultimately, practicing mindfulness and presence is about balance. For dadpreneurs, the challenge is to harmonize the demands of business with the joys of fatherhood. By embracing mindfulness, you empower yourself to be fully engaged in both endeavors. This practice not only helps in managing stress and enhancing productivity, but it also encourages a profound appreciation for the moments that matter most. As you cultivate mindfulness, you create a sustainable path towards success in your startup while cherishing the invaluable time spent with your family.

SCHEDULING QUALITY FAMILY ACTIVITIES

Scheduling quality family activities is essential for every dadpreneur striving to find harmony between the demands of a startup and the joys of family life. In the hustle of entrepreneurship, it's easy to let family time slip through the cracks, but prioritizing these moments is key to ensuring that both your business and your relationships thrive. Thoughtful scheduling fosters connection and creates lasting memories, which can serve as a powerful motivator in your entrepreneurial journey.

To effectively schedule family activities, begin by assessing your weekly routine. Identify pockets of time that can be dedicated to family without compromising your business commitments. This might mean blocking out evenings or weekends specifically for family fun. Use tools like digital calendars to set reminders for these activities, treating them with the same level of importance as business meetings. When family time is treated as a priority, it reinforces its value in your life and helps everyone stay committed to making it happen.

Consider incorporating a mix of planned outings and spontaneous activities. While having a structured schedule is beneficial, flexibility can lead to the most cherished moments. Plan a weekly family game night or a monthly outing to a local event, but also leave room for impromptu adventures. Whether it's a surprise trip to the park or a spontaneous movie night at home, these unplanned experiences can strengthen family bonds and create a sense of excitement that enriches your home life.

Involving your children in the planning process can also enhance the quality of family activities. Encourage them to suggest ideas for outings or projects, which not only makes them feel valued but also helps them develop decision-making skills. This collaborative approach fosters creativity and can lead to discovering new interests that everyone in the family can enjoy. Additionally, it teaches your kids the importance of balancing responsibilities with leisure, an essential lesson for their future.

Finally, remember that the quality of time spent together often outweighs the quantity. Focus on being fully present during family activities; put away your phone and other distractions. Engage in meaningful conversations and participate actively in the chosen activities. This dedication to quality interaction strengthens relationships and sets a positive example for your children about the importance of family in the midst of life's busyness. By scheduling quality family activities, you not only nurture your loved ones but also create a supportive environment that allows both your family and your startup to flourish.

CHAPTER 8: FINANCIAL PLANNING FOR DAD-LED STARTUPS

Budgeting for Your Startup Journey

Budgeting for your startup journey is a crucial step that can make or break your entrepreneurial aspirations. As a dadpreneur, you are already juggling multiple responsibilities, and financial management should not add to your stress. Start by defining a clear budget that aligns with both your personal and business goals. Consider your family's needs, such as childcare, education, and household expenses, while also accounting for your startup costs. By creating a comprehensive budget, you can identify how much you can invest in your business without compromising your family's financial security.

Once you have laid out your budget, prioritize your spending. Focus on essential expenses that will drive your startup forward, such as marketing, product development, and essential tools. This disciplined approach will help you avoid unnecessary expenditures and keep your financial goals in sight. It's also helpful to allocate a portion of your budget for unexpected costs, which are almost inevitable in the startup world. Setting aside a contingency fund can provide peace of mind and ensure that your entrepreneurial journey doesn't disrupt your family's financial stability.

Incorporating family into your budgeting process can foster transparency and support. Share your plans with your partner to ensure they understand your vision and the financial commitments involved. This collaboration can lead to a more robust support system, allowing both you and your partner to feel invested in the journey. Additionally, involving your children in discussions about budgeting can serve as a valuable lesson in financial literacy, teaching them about the importance of managing resources effectively.

As you progress, regularly revisit and adjust your budget to reflect changes in your business and family dynamics. Life is unpredictable, and your budget should be flexible enough to accommodate new opportunities or challenges. If your startup begins to gain traction, consider reinvesting profits into the business while maintaining a healthy work-life balance. This continuous review process will not only keep your financial goals aligned with your startup's growth but also allow you to remain present for your family.

Finally, don't underestimate the power of community and resources. As a dadpreneur, connect with other fathers in similar situations to share budgeting tips and strategies. Online forums, local meetups, or even social media groups can provide invaluable insights and support. By leveraging these networks, you can learn from others' experiences, adapt successful budgeting practices, and ultimately create a thriving startup that complements your family life rather than competes with it. Remember, a well-planned budget is not just a financial tool; it's a pathway to achieving your dreams while cherishing the moments that matter most with your family.

UNDERSTANDING BUSINESS FINANCING OPTIONS

Navigating the world of business financing can feel overwhelming, especially for dads who are balancing family responsibilities with the desire to launch a startup. However, understanding the various financing options available is crucial for transforming your entrepreneurial dreams into reality. From personal savings to loans, grants, and crowdfunding, each option has its unique advantages and considerations. As a dadpreneur, knowing how to leverage these resources can empower you to secure the necessary funds while minimizing stress and maximizing your time with family.

Personal savings often serve as the first line of defense for many aspiring business owners. Tapping into your own resources allows for full control over your venture without incurring debt. This option can be particularly appealing for busy dads who prefer a straightforward approach to funding. However, it is essential to carefully evaluate your family's financial situation. A clear budget can help you determine how much you can afford to invest without jeopardizing your family's stability, ensuring that both your business and loved ones thrive simultaneously.

If personal savings aren't sufficient, loans can provide the necessary capital to kick-start your business. Traditional bank loans, Small Business Administration (SBA) loans, and even credit union offerings are all viable paths. While loans can offer substantial funding, it's vital to approach them with caution. Dads should consider the repayment terms and interest rates, ensuring that these obligations won't interfere with family time. Additionally, preparing a solid business plan can improve your chances of securing a loan, as lenders want to see that you have a thoughtful strategy for success.

For those looking to minimize risk, grants and crowdfunding present exciting alternatives. Government grants aimed at small businesses can provide funding without the expectation of repayment, allowing you to focus on building your startup. Crowdfunding platforms allow you to present your business idea to a broader audience, garnering support from individuals who believe in your vision. This approach not only raises funds but can also create a community of supporters who may become future customers. Engaging your network and potential customers can turn financing into an opportunity to strengthen relationships and create buzz around your business.

Ultimately, the key to understanding business financing options lies in aligning your financial strategy with your family values and goals. By exploring various funding avenues, you can find the right balance that accommodates your entrepreneurial ambitions while ensuring you remain present for your family. Embrace the journey of entrepreneurship with confidence, knowing that each financing decision you make can lead to greater freedom, flexibility, and the ability to create a legacy that benefits both your business and your family.

SAVING FOR FAMILY AND BUSINESS GOALS

Saving for family and business goals is a vital aspect of any Dadpreneur's journey. As fathers striving to balance the demands of a startup with the responsibilities of family life, it's essential to create a financial roadmap that aligns with both your entrepreneurial ambitions and your family's needs. Start by identifying clear, actionable goals for your business and family. Whether it's funding your child's education, saving for a family vacation, or investing in your startup's growth, having well-defined objectives will guide your savings strategy.

Building a budget that accommodates both personal and business expenses is crucial. By tracking your income and expenditures, you can identify areas where you can cut back and allocate those savings toward your goals. Consider using technology to streamline this process—numerous apps can help you manage your finances efficiently. This not only saves you time but also allows you to stay focused on what truly matters: your family and your business. The discipline of budgeting will empower you to make informed decisions that foster growth in both areas of your life.

In addition to traditional savings, exploring alternative income streams can provide a significant boost to your financial stability. As a dadpreneur, you have unique insights into family-friendly business ideas that can generate additional revenue without sacrificing precious family time. Whether it's creating an online course, launching a subscription service, or consulting in your area of expertise, think creatively about how you can leverage your skills and passions to enhance your income. This approach not only strengthens your financial foundation but also reinforces the entrepreneurial spirit you want to instill in your children.

Networking plays an instrumental role in achieving your financial goals. Connecting with other dads who share similar aspirations can lead to valuable partnerships and collaboration opportunities. Attend local meetups, join online forums, or participate in social media groups focused on dadpreneurs. These interactions can provide insights into effective saving strategies, investment opportunities, and financial planning tailored specifically for fathers. Building a support system of like-minded individuals will not only enrich your entrepreneurial journey but also offer encouragement and motivation along the way.

Ultimately, the journey of saving for family and business goals is about more than just numbers; it's about creating a legacy of resilience and ambition for your children. As you work toward achieving financial success, ensure you involve your family in the process. Share your goals with them, involve them in discussions about budgeting, and celebrate milestones together. By modeling financial responsibility and entrepreneurial spirit, you'll inspire your children to pursue their passions while understanding the importance of balancing work and family life. This approach will not only strengthen your family bonds but also equip the next generation for their own journeys as they navigate the world of business and beyond.

CHAPTER 9: MARKETING STRATEGIES FOR DADPRENEURS

Identifying Your Target Audience

Identifying your target audience is a crucial step for any dadpreneur embarking on the journey of building a startup while juggling family responsibilities. As a father, you naturally understand the importance of connecting with others who share similar experiences. This shared understanding creates a strong foundation for a community where busy dads can support each other. Recognizing who your audience is will not only help you tailor your products or services to meet their needs but also foster lasting relationships that can enhance both your business and personal life.

Start by considering the unique challenges faced by fathers who are striving to balance family life with entrepreneurial pursuits. Many dads are looking for ways to create additional income streams without sacrificing precious time with their children. This demographic includes busy professionals aiming to transition from a corporate job to a more flexible and fulfilling business model. By honing in on these specific pain points, you can develop solutions that resonate deeply with your audience, whether that's through family-friendly business ideas or effective time management strategies designed for dadpreneurs.

Next, think about the niches that are most relevant to your target audience. For instance, many fathers are eager to learn about setting up a home office that accommodates both work and family life. This can include tips on creating a productive workspace that minimizes distractions while being family-friendly. Additionally, offering insights into financial planning for dad-led startups can be incredibly valuable, as many fathers are concerned about managing their finances while pursuing entrepreneurial ventures. Understanding these niches will allow you to create targeted content that speaks directly to the needs of your audience.

Networking is another vital aspect of identifying your target audience. Many dadpreneurs benefit from connecting with other fathers who are on similar journeys. By creating opportunities for networking, whether through online platforms or local meetups, you can build a community where dads share parenting tips, marketing strategies, and work-life balance techniques. Encouraging collaboration and support among fathers not only strengthens individual businesses but also fosters a sense of camaraderie that is essential for overcoming the challenges of entrepreneurship.

Finally, leverage technology to reach your target audience effectively. Utilize social media, blogs, and podcasts to share your insights and experiences as a dadpreneur. By doing so, you can establish yourself as a thought leader in the space while also creating valuable resources for your audience. This connection through technology allows for flexibility, enabling fathers to engage with your content during their limited free time. Ultimately, identifying and understanding your target audience will empower you to create a thriving business that harmoniously coexists with your family life, turning your entrepreneurial dreams into reality.

BUILDING A BRAND THAT RESONATES

Building a brand that resonates is essential for any dadpreneur striving to carve out a niche in the competitive world of startups. As fathers juggling business ambitions and family obligations, it is crucial to create a brand identity that reflects both your personal values and your family-oriented approach. When your brand captures the essence of who you are as a dad and an entrepreneur, it becomes a compelling story that resonates with your target audience. This authenticity not only fosters trust but also builds an emotional connection with potential customers who see their own struggles and aspirations reflected in your brand.

To build a brand that resonates, start by identifying your core values. Consider what matters most to you as a father and an entrepreneur. Are you passionate about creating innovative products that simplify family life? Do you want to promote work-life balance as a central tenet of your business philosophy? By defining these values, you establish a foundation for your brand that speaks to your audience's needs and desires. This clarity will guide your branding decisions, helping you choose colors, fonts, and messaging that align with your mission and resonate with busy dads seeking solutions.

Storytelling is a powerful tool in branding, especially for dadpreneurs. Sharing your journey as a father and entrepreneur allows your audience to connect with your experiences on a personal level. Use your brand's platform to narrate the challenges you've faced, the lessons learned, and the triumphs achieved while balancing family life and business pursuits. By being open and relatable, you create an authentic narrative that not only captivates but also inspires other fathers. This storytelling approach reinforces your brand identity and cultivates a community of like-minded individuals who rally around your mission.

In addition to storytelling, leverage digital marketing strategies to amplify your brand's reach. Social media platforms provide an excellent avenue for engaging with your audience and sharing valuable content that speaks to their needs. Create content that addresses the intersection of family and entrepreneurship, such as time management tips, practical home office setups, or innovative family-friendly business ideas. By positioning yourself as a thought leader in these areas, you not only enhance your brand's visibility but also establish credibility and trust among your audience.

Finally, remember that building a brand is an ongoing process that requires adaptability and responsiveness. As your business grows and evolves, so too should your brand. Stay attuned to the feedback from your audience and be willing to pivot your messaging or offerings as needed. By remaining flexible and open to change, you ensure that your brand continues to resonate with your target market. Ultimately, a brand that authentically reflects your values and connects with your audience will not only foster business success but also create a legacy that positively impacts your family and community.

UTILIZING SOCIAL MEDIA AND CONTENT MARKETING

In the digital age, social media and content marketing have become essential tools for entrepreneurs, especially for dadpreneurs navigating the dual responsibilities of family and business. By harnessing these platforms, you can connect with your target audience, share your story, and establish your brand without compromising precious family time. The beauty of social media lies in its accessibility and potential for engagement, allowing you to build a community around your startup while still being present for your children. The key is to create a strategic approach that aligns with your family values and business goals.

Content marketing allows you to showcase your expertise and build trust among potential customers. This is particularly vital for dadpreneurs, who often juggle multiple roles. By sharing valuable insights through blogs, videos, or podcasts, you not only position yourself as a knowledgeable leader in your niche but also create a resource that others can turn to. Whether you're offering parenting tips or time management strategies, each piece of content helps to humanize your brand and resonate with fellow fathers who share your challenges and aspirations.

Social media platforms provide an incredible opportunity to amplify your content and reach a broader audience. By utilizing platforms like Instagram, Facebook, and LinkedIn, you can engage with your followers in real-time, creating meaningful interactions that deepen relationships. Share snippets of your daily life as a dadpreneur, behind-the-scenes looks at your startup journey, or even quick tips for balancing work and family. This not only fosters a connection with your audience but also encourages them to share your content, expanding your reach organically.

To maximize your efforts, consider creating a content calendar that balances promotional posts with personal stories and educational resources. This structured approach ensures that you remain consistent without feeling overwhelmed. Allocate specific times during your week for content creation and engagement, allowing you to manage your time effectively. Remember, your family should always come first, so find ways to involve them in your content. This could mean sharing family-friendly business ideas or even collaborating with your kids in your social media content, showcasing the harmony between your entrepreneurial journey and family life.

Ultimately, utilizing social media and content marketing is about crafting a narrative that reflects your values as both a father and an entrepreneur. By being authentic and relatable, you not only attract customers but also build a community of like-minded individuals who inspire and support one another. Embrace this journey, and remember that every post, every piece of content, and every interaction is a step toward achieving your goals while nurturing the family bond that fuels your passion.

CHAPTER 10: LEVERAGING TECHNOLOGY TO MANAGE BUSINESS AND FAMILY

Tools for Project Management

In the journey of building a startup while nurturing family relationships, having the right tools for project management can make all the difference. For dadpreneurs, juggling both worlds requires a strategic approach, and the right tools can help you streamline tasks, prioritize effectively, and maintain a clear focus on what truly matters. Imagine a system that not only keeps your business organized but also allows you to be present for your family. This is where project management tools come into play, offering solutions that cater specifically to the needs of busy fathers.

First and foremost, task management software like Trello or Asana can transform the way you handle daily responsibilities. These platforms enable you to create boards or lists that represent your projects and their individual tasks. As a dadpreneur, you can set deadlines, assign tasks, and even track progress in real-time. This visibility not only helps you stay accountable but also allows you to carve out dedicated time for family activities. By visualizing your workload, you can avoid the overwhelm that often comes with balancing a startup and family life.

Collaboration is another vital aspect of project management that can enhance both your business and family dynamics. Tools like Slack or Microsoft Teams foster communication among team members, whether they are employees or family members involved in your entrepreneurial journey. Keeping everyone in the loop ensures that work progresses smoothly and that any issues are addressed promptly. This communal approach can also inspire your children to participate in age-appropriate tasks, fostering a sense of teamwork and responsibility within the family unit.

Time tracking tools such as Clockify or Toggl empower you to understand where your hours are going. For dadpreneurs, seeing how much time is devoted to various tasks can reveal opportunities to optimize your schedule. Are you spending too much time on administrative duties? Are there aspects of your business that could be automated? By identifying these patterns, you can allocate more time to family activities, ensuring that you're not just a dad in name but also in presence. This balance is crucial in building strong connections with your loved ones while pursuing your entrepreneurial dreams.

Finally, a good project management tool should integrate seamlessly with other technology you use, from calendars to email platforms. Utilizing tools like Notion or ClickUp can centralize your business activities, making it easier to manage your time and commitments. With everything in one place, you can quickly shift from business tasks to family time without losing momentum. This integration not only enhances productivity but also allows you to set clear boundaries between work and home life, a cornerstone of successful dadpreneurship.

Embracing these project management tools not only equips you to tackle the challenges of entrepreneurship but also ensures that your family remains a priority. As you build your startup, remember that your role as a father is just as significant as your role as an entrepreneur. By leveraging the right resources, you can create a thriving business while nurturing a loving and supportive family environment, proving that success is not solely measured by financial gain but by the quality of time spent with those you cherish.

APPS FOR FAMILY ORGANIZATION

In the whirlwind of family life and startup ambitions, finding the right tools to keep everything organized can be a game changer for Dadpreneurs. Apps designed for family organization not only streamline daily tasks but also foster a sense of togetherness amidst the chaos of juggling a business and family responsibilities. By leveraging technology, fathers can create a more harmonious home environment, allowing them to focus on nurturing their entrepreneurial dreams while ensuring quality time with their loved ones.

One of the most effective ways to manage family schedules and activities is through shared calendar applications. These platforms enable dads to synchronize their commitments with their partners and children, ensuring everyone is on the same page. Whether it's soccer practice, school events, or important business meetings, a shared calendar helps prevent scheduling conflicts and reduces the stress of last-minute changes. By assigning color codes for different family members, dads can visually track who needs to be where and when, making it easier to plan family outings or business commitments.

Task management apps are another powerful tool for Dadpreneurs striving to balance their diverse roles. These applications allow fathers to create to-do lists that can include both personal and professional tasks, helping them prioritize their time effectively. By breaking down larger projects into manageable steps, dads can tackle their business goals while also completing household chores or planning family activities. Some apps even include features for delegation, enabling fathers to share tasks with spouses or older children, fostering teamwork and responsibility within the family.

Moreover, meal planning apps can significantly reduce the time spent on grocery shopping and cooking, which can often be a source of stress for busy fathers. By organizing weekly meals, these apps help Dadpreneurs save time and ensure that their families are eating healthy. Many of these platforms offer recipe suggestions based on dietary preferences and include grocery lists that simplify shopping. When meal prep becomes effortless, it frees up precious hours that dads can dedicate to their startups or family bonding activities, reinforcing the idea that a well-fed family is a happy family.

Finally, communication apps serve as a vital link between family members and their various activities. Whether through group messaging or shared notes, these tools enhance connectivity and ensure that everyone is informed and involved in family planning. By establishing open lines of communication, Dadpreneurs can engage their children in discussions about business ventures or upcoming family events, making them feel valued and included in the entrepreneurial journey. Together, these apps create a supportive ecosystem that empowers fathers to thrive in both their personal and professional lives, ultimately leading to a more fulfilling and balanced existence.

BALANCING SCREEN TIME WITH FAMILY ENGAGEMENT

In today's digital world, finding the right balance between screen time and family engagement is crucial for dadpreneurs. As fathers embarking on the startup journey, it can be easy to become absorbed in the demands of your business, especially when technology offers endless distractions. However, it's essential to prioritize quality time with your family to foster strong relationships and create a supportive home environment. By intentionally managing screen time, you can cultivate a deeper connection with your loved ones while still pursuing your entrepreneurial dreams.

Establishing boundaries around screen time is a foundational step for any dadpreneur. Designate specific hours for work-related tasks and ensure these do not encroach upon family time. For instance, set aside certain evenings or weekends for uninterrupted family activities. This approach not only enhances your productivity during work hours but also allows you to engage fully with your family when it matters most. By communicating these boundaries to your family, you can create a culture of mutual respect and understanding, reinforcing the idea that both work and family time are valuable.

Incorporating technology in a family-friendly way can also enhance engagement. Use tech tools to organize family activities or create a shared calendar that includes both business commitments and family events. Encourage your kids to participate in tech-related projects that align with your business, allowing them to feel involved and valued. By integrating your entrepreneurial journey into family life, you not only inspire your children but also create lasting memories that reinforce your family bond. The key is to choose activities that are inclusive and enjoyable for everyone, making technology a tool for connection rather than a barrier.

Mindfulness is another essential aspect of balancing screen time with family engagement. Practicing mindfulness helps you become aware of when technology is taking over and when it's time to unplug. Simple strategies like setting aside devices during meals or designating tech-free zones in the home can create spaces for meaningful conversations and interactions. Encourage everyone to engage in activities that promote presence, such as board games, outdoor adventures, or family projects. This shift in focus from screens to shared experiences can rejuvenate your family dynamics and foster deeper connections.

Ultimately, balancing screen time with family engagement isn't just about limiting device usage; it's about cultivating a mindset that values presence and connection. As a dadpreneur, your journey is unique, and the lessons you learn along the way can shape the future of your family. Embrace the challenge of finding harmony between your entrepreneurial aspirations and your role as a father. By prioritizing family engagement, you will not only enhance your startup success but also create a legacy of love, support, and resilience for your children to inherit.

CHAPTER 11: PERSONAL DEVELOPMENT FOR ENTREPRENEURIAL FATHERS

Setting Personal and Professional Goals

Setting personal and professional goals is a crucial aspect of any dadpreneur's journey. The dual responsibilities of nurturing a family and building a startup can feel overwhelming, but having clear, actionable goals can transform that chaos into a structured path forward. Start by envisioning what success looks like for you, both as a father and as a business owner. This vision will serve as a guiding light, helping you navigate the demands of family life while pursuing your entrepreneurial dreams. Write down your aspirations, whether they involve financial milestones, work-life harmony, or personal growth, to create a tangible roadmap for your journey.

Once you have your vision in place, break it down into smaller, achievable goals. This is where the power of specificity comes into play. Instead of setting a vague goal like "be successful in business," aim for concrete targets, such as launching your product within six months or securing your first five customers. By defining these milestones, you create opportunities for regular reflection and adjustment, allowing you to stay focused and motivated. Celebrating small wins along the way not only boosts your morale but also reinforces the importance of your dual commitments to family and entrepreneurship.

In the midst of your busy life, it is essential to prioritize your goals effectively. Time management strategies will be your best friend. Allocate specific time blocks for family activities and work tasks, ensuring that each area receives the attention it deserves. Use tools like calendars and to-do lists to keep track of your commitments and deadlines. This structure will not only enhance your productivity but will also help you to create boundaries, ensuring that your work does not encroach on precious family moments. Remember, being present with your family is as important as being productive in your business.

Moreover, leverage technology to streamline your efforts in both realms. Numerous apps and platforms can assist in managing tasks, tracking progress, and even facilitating communication with your family. Setting up a dedicated home office equipped with the right tools will create an environment conducive to focus and creativity. This intentional setup allows you to separate work from personal life physically, making it easier to switch gears when needed. Embrace these resources to help you balance your responsibilities more effectively, allowing you to devote quality time to both your startup and your loved ones.

Finally, don't underestimate the value of support and networking. Connect with other dadpreneurs who understand the unique challenges you face. Sharing experiences, advice, and encouragement can provide a much-needed boost on tough days. Attend local meetups or online forums where you can discuss strategies and learn from others' successes and setbacks. Building a community around your ambitions not only enhances your knowledge but also reinforces your commitment to achieving your goals. By setting clear personal and professional goals, prioritizing effectively, leveraging technology, and seeking support, you can navigate the rewarding yet complex journey of being a dadpreneur while ensuring that your family remains at the heart of your endeavors.

CONTINUOUS LEARNING AND SKILL DEVELOPMENT

Continuous learning and skill development are essential components of a successful journey for any dadpreneur. As you navigate the complexities of building a startup while fulfilling your family obligations, embracing a mindset of lifelong learning can empower you to adapt to challenges, seize new opportunities, and ultimately thrive. In the fast-paced world of entrepreneurship, the ability to continuously acquire knowledge and skills not only enhances your professional capacity but also sets a powerful example for your children, showing them the value of growth and resilience.

Incorporating learning into your daily routine is crucial, especially when time is limited. Consider dedicating small pockets of time throughout your day to enhance your skills. Whether it's listening to podcasts during your commute, watching online courses while your children nap, or reading books at the end of the day, these moments can cumulatively lead to significant growth. Furthermore, seeking out family-friendly learning opportunities can create bonding experiences with your kids. Involve them in projects that align with your business goals, fostering their curiosity while reinforcing your commitment to both family and entrepreneurship.

Networking is another vital aspect of skill development for dadpreneurs. Engaging with fellow entrepreneurs provides not just support but also invaluable insights and knowledge sharing. Attend local meetups, join online forums, and participate in workshops designed for fathers in business. These connections can open doors to mentorship opportunities, collaborations, and even potential partnerships. Surrounding yourself with like-minded individuals can inspire you to pursue new ideas and keep your motivation high, reminding you that you are not alone in this journey.

Embracing technology can significantly enhance your learning and skill development efforts. Leverage online platforms that offer courses tailored to your needs. From marketing strategies to financial planning, there is a wealth of information available at your fingertips. Technology also allows for flexibility, enabling you to learn at your own pace. Utilize apps that help you manage your time effectively, ensuring that you can balance your personal development with family commitments. This integration of tech into your learning journey can streamline your processes, giving you more quality time with your loved ones.

Ultimately, committing to continuous learning and skill development is about more than just professional growth; it's about modeling a growth mindset for your children. As you pursue your entrepreneurial dreams, you instill in them the importance of adaptability, perseverance, and lifelong learning. By balancing your startup ambitions with family life, you create an environment where both you and your children can thrive together. The journey may be challenging, but the rewards of personal and professional growth enrich not just your life but your family's future as well.

FINDING INSPIRATION AND MOTIVATION

Finding inspiration and motivation as a dadpreneur can often feel like a daunting task, especially when juggling the complexities of family life and the demands of a startup. However, tapping into the unique blend of your roles as a father and an entrepreneur can provide a wellspring of motivation. Consider the dreams and aspirations you hold for your family; these visions can ignite a fire within you. Each time you think about the legacy you want to leave or the financial stability you aim to provide, you can transform those thoughts into actionable goals that inspire you to push through challenges.

Surrounding yourself with a supportive network is another crucial aspect of finding inspiration. Engage with other fathers who share your entrepreneurial dreams. Their experiences, advice, and encouragement can serve as a powerful source of motivation. Online forums, local meetups, or social media groups dedicated to dadpreneurs can offer not just networking opportunities but also a sense of camaraderie. Sharing both victories and struggles can provide insights and perspectives that fuel your drive to succeed.

Incorporating daily routines that prioritize both business and family can also help maintain motivation. Set aside specific times for family activities, ensuring that these moments are cherished and celebrated. When you allocate time to connect with your children, it can serve as a refreshing reminder of why you embarked on this entrepreneurial journey in the first place. Balancing your schedule with intention allows you to see the fruits of your labor in both your personal and professional life, reinforcing your commitment to both roles.

Adopting a growth mindset is essential for staying motivated during the inevitable ups and downs of entrepreneurship. Embrace challenges as opportunities for learning and growth. Each setback can teach valuable lessons, shaping you into a more resilient person and entrepreneur. Approach each obstacle with curiosity rather than fear, and celebrate the small victories along the way. Recognizing and appreciating progress, however minor, can invigorate your spirit and keep you focused on your long-term goals.

Lastly, never underestimate the power of self-care in maintaining your drive. As a dadpreneur, it's easy to become consumed by work and family responsibilities, but taking time for yourself is vital. Whether it's exercising, pursuing a hobby, or simply enjoying a quiet moment with a book, these activities can recharge your mental and emotional batteries. Remember, a well-rested and fulfilled dad is more equipped to inspire and lead both his family and his business. By prioritizing your well-being, you not only enhance your own motivation but also model healthy habits for your children, ensuring they see the importance of balance in life.

CHAPTER 12: CELEBRATING YOUR SUCCESSES AND ADJUSTING GOALS

Reflecting on Achievements

Reflecting on achievements is a crucial practice for dadpreneurs striving to balance the demands of family life and the challenges of building a successful startup. Amidst the hustle of juggling parenting duties, business meetings, and a myriad of responsibilities, it is easy to overlook the milestones that mark progress. Taking the time to acknowledge these achievements not only reinforces your commitment to your goals but also provides the motivation needed to push through obstacles. Each small victory, whether it's landing a new client or spending quality time with your children, deserves recognition as a significant step forward in your journey.

As you reflect on your accomplishments, consider the unique milestones that come with being both a father and a budding entrepreneur. Perhaps you successfully implemented a new time management strategy that allowed you to dedicate more evenings to family dinners, or you launched a family-friendly business idea that aligns with your values. Each achievement contributes to a larger narrative of balancing family and business, demonstrating that success can be defined in various ways. Celebrating these moments can foster a sense of fulfillment, reminding you that you are not just building a business, but also creating a legacy for your children.

Moreover, acknowledging your achievements can serve as a powerful tool for personal development. When you take the time to reflect, you can identify patterns in your success that may lead to further growth. Understanding what worked well allows you to replicate those strategies, while recognizing setbacks can guide you in making necessary adjustments. This reflection helps you evolve as both a dad and an entrepreneur, cultivating resilience and adaptability—qualities essential for navigating the unpredictable landscape of startup life.

Involving your family in this reflective process can deepen your connection and instill values of perseverance and gratitude in your children. Share your successes with them, no matter how small, and encourage their participation in celebrating these achievements. Not only does this create a supportive environment, but it also teaches your kids the importance of recognizing hard work and determination. In doing so, you model a healthy relationship with success that emphasizes the value of effort over mere outcomes, nurturing their aspirations as they grow.

Ultimately, reflecting on achievements is not merely about recognizing past successes but also about setting the stage for future triumphs. By taking stock of what you've accomplished, you can create a vision for your next steps—whether that's scaling your business, exploring new income streams, or enhancing your work-life balance. This practice fosters a growth mindset, empowering you to embrace challenges as opportunities. As you continue your journey as a dadpreneur, remember that each achievement, no matter how small, is a building block towards a fulfilling life that harmonizes family commitment with entrepreneurial ambition.

ADAPTING TO LIFE'S CHANGES

Adapting to life's changes is an essential skill for every dadpreneur determined to navigate the intricate landscape of family life and entrepreneurial aspirations. The reality is that life is rarely predictable, and the journey of building a startup often comes with unexpected twists and turns. Embracing these changes with a positive mindset is crucial. Rather than viewing obstacles as setbacks, consider them opportunities for growth. Each challenge faced can lead to new insights, whether it's learning to manage your time more effectively or finding innovative solutions to problems that arise in both family and business.

Flexibility becomes your greatest ally in this journey. As a dadpreneur, you will quickly discover that your plans may need to shift, sometimes at a moment's notice. Children get sick, work demands fluctuate, and personal commitments arise. Developing a flexible mindset allows you to pivot without losing sight of your goals. Establish routines that can adapt to changing circumstances. For instance, setting aside specific times during the week for family and business activities can create a structure while still allowing for spontaneity when life calls for it.

Communication plays a pivotal role in adapting to changes. Open dialogue with your family about your entrepreneurial journey can foster understanding and support. Share your aspirations, challenges, and the reasons behind your decisions. This transparency not only strengthens family bonds but also encourages your children to embrace their own challenges. By modeling resilience and adaptability, you teach valuable life lessons that extend beyond the realm of business, instilling a sense of perseverance and creativity in your children.

Creating a support system is another essential aspect of adaptation. As you embark on this entrepreneurial path, surround yourself with individuals who understand your journey —other dadpreneurs, mentors, or business networks can provide invaluable insights and encouragement. These connections can help you navigate the complexities of balancing family and business. They may offer practical advice on time management or share their experiences in overcoming similar hurdles, making your own transition smoother and more informed.

Lastly, embracing self-care and personal development is vital as you adapt to life's changes. Prioritize your well-being to ensure you have the energy and focus to tackle both family responsibilities and business challenges. Engage in activities that rejuvenate you, whether it's exercise, reading, or spending quality time with your family. Investing in your personal growth not only benefits you but also enhances your ability to lead your family and your business effectively. Remember, the journey of a dadpreneur is not merely about achieving business success; it's also about nurturing a fulfilling family life, and adapting to change is at the heart of that balance.

PLANNING FOR THE FUTURE WITH CONFIDENCE

Planning for the future with confidence is essential for any dadpreneur striving to create a successful business while nurturing family life. Embracing the dual role of father and entrepreneur can feel daunting, but with the right mindset and strategies, you can chart a course that allows you to achieve your goals without sacrificing precious family time. Understanding that the future is not merely a series of events waiting to unfold, but a canvas that you can actively shape, empowers you to take charge of your journey as both a dad and a business owner.

To begin this journey, set clear, realistic goals for your business and family life. Consider what success looks like for you—whether it means reaching a specific revenue target, launching a new product, or simply having more time to spend with your kids. By identifying these key objectives, you can create a roadmap that aligns your business ambitions with your family values. Break these goals down into actionable steps, ensuring that you regularly assess your progress. This proactive approach not only fosters a sense of achievement but also reinforces your commitment to your family's well-being.

Time management becomes your greatest ally in this balancing act. As a dadpreneur, it's crucial to carve out dedicated time for both work and family. Utilize tools and techniques such as time blocking or the Pomodoro Technique to maintain focus and productivity during work hours. Additionally, establish family rituals that create quality moments together, whether it's a weekly game night or a Sunday outing. This structured approach allows you to compartmentalize your responsibilities, ensuring that neither your business nor your family feels neglected, and instills a sense of order in your life.

Networking is another vital component of planning for the future with confidence. Build relationships with fellow dadpreneurs, mentors, and industry experts who can provide guidance, support, and potential collaboration opportunities. Attend local meetups or online forums specifically designed for entrepreneurial fathers, where you can share experiences and learn from one another. These connections can open doors to new ideas and partnerships, benefiting both your business and your personal growth. Remember, you are not alone in this journey; a strong network can offer encouragement and inspiration when you need it most.

Lastly, embrace the power of technology to streamline both your business operations and family interactions. Use apps for project management, time tracking, and communication to keep everything organized and efficient. Leverage digital tools to maintain family calendars and schedules, ensuring that everyone is on the same page. By harnessing technology, you can reduce stress and free up valuable time to focus on what truly matters —being present for your family while building the future you envision for them. With confidence and clarity in your planning, you can navigate the challenges of dadpreneurship and create a fulfilling life that honors both your entrepreneurial dreams and your role as a devoted father.

This guide is provided for informational purposes only and reflects the author's experiences and insights on balancing entrepreneurship with family life. Readers should consult with professional advisors for business-specific advice.

ENTREPRENEURSHIP VIBES

Entrepreneurship Vibes is a dynamic book series designed for today's entrepreneurs who want to make their mark in the digital age. Whether you're starting your first business, scaling your side hustle, or navigating the challenges of growth, this series breaks down the essential strategies, tools, and mindset shifts you need to succeed.

Each volume focuses on different facets of entrepreneurship, including goal-setting, productivity hacks, digital marketing mastery, and the art of balancing work-life demands. Packed with real-life examples, actionable steps, and expert advice, Entrepreneurship Vibes offers both inspiration and practical guidance.

If you're a visionary seeking financial independence, generational wealth, or simply a more fulfilling career, this series is your go-to roadmap. Unlock your potential, vibe with success, and step into the world of limitless possibilities.

Mastering The Art Of Financial Independence: : The Journey To Financial Freedom – Your Blueprint For Building Generational Wealth

Greetings, fellow adventurers and wealth builders! If you're reading this, you're likely standing at the crossroads of aspiration and reality, ready to pivot toward financial freedom. This guide is crafted just for you.
Here, you'll find not just strategies, but stories of resilience,

adaptability, and practical steps that have propelled others, just like you, from blue-collar diligence to digital empire builders.

Social Media Mastery: Unlocking Entrepreneurial Growth Through Digital Platforms

In today's fast-paced digital landscape, social media is a driving force behind entrepreneurial growth. Whether you're a new startup or an established business, mastering social media platforms like Instagram, Facebook, and LinkedIn is critical to engaging with customers and expanding your reach. With the right strategy, social media provides unparalleled opportunities to create a loyal audience, generate leads, and drive sales—all while building your brand's identity and community.

"Social Media Mastery" is your ultimate guide to unlocking the full potential of digital platforms for entrepreneurial success. This comprehensive book dives deep into actionable strategies that every business owner needs to leverage social media channels like Facebook, Instagram, LinkedIn, and TikTok. Whether you're looking to grow your brand, generate leads, or build a community, this book provides the insights you need to craft engaging content, run effective ad campaigns, and foster meaningful connections with your audience.

Inside, you'll discover tips on content creation, how to build a consistent brand voice, and advanced advertising techniques. From understanding your target audience to building authentic relationships through influencer marketing, every chapter is filled with examples, tools, and proven methods to help you navigate the ever-changing world of social media.

www.ingramcontent.com/pod-product-compliance
Lightning Source LLC
Chambersburg PA
CBHW070353230526
45471CB00006B/2548